THE
STOCK MARKET
INVESTING GUIDE
FOR BEGINNERS

The Intelligent Investor Guide: How to Invest in Stocks, Build Sustainable Cashflow and Generate Wealth incl. Stocks, ETFs and More

KENNETH ANDERSON

TABLE OF CONTENTS

INTRODUCTION

'How many millionaires do you know who have become wealthy by investing in savings accounts? I rest my case.'

(Personal finance guru Robert G. Allen)

When it comes to investing, you have so many options. It can be confusing!

What do people mean when they say 'invest in the stock market'?

Globally, there are over 60 stock markets. Investing in the stock markets — strictly speaking — means investing in stocks. Each stock means you get a share in the total value of a company. The price of that share goes up and down according to how the company is seen to be performing.

But nowadays, when people say they are 'investing in the stock market' they might mean a whole lot more than investing in stocks. With an online stockbroker you can invest in:

- ☑ **Commodities**: material products like oil, grain and precious metals.

- ☑ **Bonds:** financial contracts that go up and down in value, and tend to do well when the stock market is not doing well. Bonds are great low-risk investments.

- ☑ **Funds:** pools of different assets which you can buy into. Some funds are run by fund managers. Some are not. Index funds and ETFs (Exchange Traded Funds) are examples of funds. ETFs are great for beginners.

- ☑ **Cryptocurrencies:** digital currencies which usually relate to new technologies in how businesses and people exchange value safely and anonymously. A Wild West market!

- ☑ **CFDs, or 'Contracts For Difference':** CFDs are products which allow you invest in products without actually owning the underlying asset. CFDs allow private investors access to all sorts of markets which used to be the sole preserve of investment professionals.

☑ **Options:** complicated contracts which allow you to invest in the future price of particular products. Not for beginners!

☑ **Alternative Investments:** invest in private companies, hedge funds, crowdfunding, art and antiques, real estate. Strictly speaking, all investments that are not stocks, bonds or cash are alternative investments.

What's the most important thing to know about the stock markets?

You will have heard of stock market crashes. Like the Wall Street Crash of 1929 that caused the Great Depression. Or the Financial Crisis of 2007-2008. There are plenty more such crashes throughout history.

Forget about the crashes! What you need to get straight is that, despite crashes, stock markets rise in value over time. They always have done. They have odd years when their value decreases: these are called 'bear' markets. And they have years when their value increases dramatically: these are called 'bull' markets. But generally the movement of stock markets is up.

BULL MARKET? BEAR MARKET?

In a bull market, prices go up. In a bear market, prices go down. Where do these animal associations come from? Nobody is certain. But one simple explanation is that bulls attack by sweeping their horns up, so they are associated with markets moving upwards. And bears attack by swiping downwards with their paws, so they are associated with markets going down in value.

A more complicated explanation for the term 'bear' market derives from an 18th century British proverb 'don't sell the bearskin before you have caught the bear'. Selling the bearskin without a bear is effectively what traders are doing when they 'go short' on a market: they sell borrowed stock (ie. the 'bearskin without the bear') in the belief that the stock will fall in value and they can then buy the stock at a reduced price.

The movement of stock markets is tracked by indexes. The best-known index globally is the *S&P 500* Index, which tracks the performance of 500 large US companies. You can invest in indices (plural of 'index') directly via ETFs.

Since its inception in 1928, the S&P 500 Index has grown in value by an astonishing 22,000%.

That is not a typo. $100 invested back in 1928 would be worth $2,200,000 now.

What this means is that one certain way of making money in the stock markets is to invest in decent companies and let time do the rest. That is why 55% of US citizens have money invested in the stock market. Because, provided you do not get too ambitious, you can put the money in and generate wealth without lifting a finger.

If you are in a hurry to make money, there are plenty of strategies and markets where the gains are quicker and more dramatic. But, where the gains are higher, the risks are higher. The choice is yours. Your financial future lies in your own hands. You just need to be armed with the facts before you go plunging in.

How do stock markets work?

Stock markets differ from conventional markets in that you can sell as well as buy goods). You buy and sell stocks (as well as bonds) via an online broker, who makes money by sometimes charging fees and commissions. Brokers usually make money too by offering a 'spread' between the price you can buy at and the price you can sell at.

Your online broker records your purchases in your own stock portfolio. You can review this online.

The largest stock exchange in the world is the New York Stock Exchange (NYSE). Founded in 1792, this exchange trades in stocks of 2,800 US companies, and has a market capitalisation of over $26 trillion. 'Market capitalisation' here means the total value of all financial assets traded.

Founded in 1971, the NASDAQ is the second-biggest exchange in the world with a market capitalisation of over $15 trillion. The NASDAQ features US stocks with a heavy tech bias.

The London Stock Exchange is the UK's biggest stock exchange. It is often referred to as the FTSE (Financial Times Stock Exchange), or 'footsie' for short, because the dominant index is the FTSE 100, which lists the biggest 100 stocks listed.

Companies can choose which stock exchanges they want to be listed on, provided they can meet the exchange's requirements.

Why do companies get listed on stock exchanges and sell shares?

Companies sell shares to raise money. They use this money to invest in themselves and therefore hope to make more money. When companies issue shares to be bought by private and institutional investors, they go through a process called an Initial Public Offering (IPO). This IPO is organised by one or more investment banks, who ensure that shares get listed on stock exchanges.

So can we get started investing now?

The principle of a stock market is easy enough to understand. But there are many other related financial markets where you can buy assets other than stocks and bonds. To know what assets are right for you, we need to start at the beginning of your story.

So, in this book you will:

- ☑ Start by building your own simple investment plan. That begins by establishing your 'risk appetite' – which means how much financial risk is appropriate to your life situation.

- ☑ Then you will review what financial assets are available to invest in. Each comes with a different risk profile.

- ☑ Then you will review how different investment strategies match your risk appetite with suitable assets.

☑ Next, you will dive into the practicalities of how online brokers work. Learn what to look for, and pick the right broker for you.

☑ You will pick up expert tips.

☑ You will review the world's top 5 investors, and grasp in simple terms what their strategies were.

☑ You will learn from the mistakes of when investing has gone horribly wrong in the past.

☑ You will crunch investment jargon.

HOW DO I GET STARTED IN INVESTING?

'Is what you are doing today getting you closer to where you want to be tomorrow?'

(Anonymous)

4 simple steps to start investing

1. Write a simple investment plan ...

2. Get on your mobile phone or computer ...

3. Find a reputable broker ...

4. Allocate some funds from your bank — and get investing!

What is my investment plan?

Your investment plan is a simple document that you write yourself. You do not have to be a genius at writing: your investment plan should fit onto a single page. Keep it simple.

To complete your investment plan, you need to answer four questions:

1. **What personal factors play into my investment plan?**
   Two questions apply here: i) How old are you? If you are young, you can invest how you like. If you are getting older, options become more limited: you may need to consider investment strategies with higher risk profiles. Question ii) what capital do you have to start with? You do not need much to get going with stock market investing. Online stockbrokers offering minimum deposits as low as $100 (or €100 /£100). But remember that some fees will apply as you go along. A reasonable sum to get started with investing is more like $500.

2. **What goal do I want to achieve with investment?**
   Are you investing to get rich generally? Or maybe you are investing for your own retirement? Maybe you are investing to look after your family in the

future? Whatever your investment goal is, do not be afraid to get it down on paper as simply as possible. You need to be clear and honest from the outset (and maybe the investment gods will smile on you!). Clarifying *why* you are investing will make choosing your risk appetite and investment strategy easier.

3. **What 'risk appetite' do I have as an investor?** Investors are classified as having a 'risk appetite'. This can be low, medium, or high. If you want to hang onto your money at all costs, you have a low risk appetite. If you are prepared to take some risks, but want to try and generally stay steady, you have a medium appetite for risk. If you are prepared to go all out and risk losing the farm, you have a high risk appetite. Most investors have a medium risk appetite: nobody wants to lose money, but nobody wants to lose out on opportunities either.

4. **How am I going to achieve my investment goal?** This is where you commit to paper which investment strategy you are going to stick to. It helps to write it down. We will look at investment strategies after we have reviewed which financial assets are available to invest in.

TOP TIP:

Investment products are often referred to as having a 'risk profile'. This corresponds to an investor's risk appetite. So, for example, a product with a low risk profile (like government bonds) would suit an investor with a low risk appetite. Products with a high risk profile (like cryptocurrencies) would suit an investor with a high risk appetite.

Why do I need an investment plan?

Unless you have an investment plan, you will fall into the biggest newbie trap. This is the trap of human emotion. Investment is not about emotion. It is about logic. Write your plan down, and you will be less likely to be swept away by emotion in the future.

Can I practice investing without losing any money?

Yes. Most online brokers offer demo accounts where you can experiment with pretend money and build a virtual portfolio.

Can I learn more about investing for free?

Yes. Many brokers are offering 'social trading' online. This means their brokerage site has loads of chatrooms, forums and newsfeeds where you can talk to other investors and pick up tips.

Can I copy more experienced investors?

Yes. Along with social trading, a new development with some brokers is 'copy trading'. This allows you to exactly copy what other traders are doing. Usually, brokers will not charge for the copying itself – but you will get charged any commissions that apply to the trades you carry out.

What is great about copy trading is that usually the broker's software will do it all for you. You simply allocate as many funds as you want to be involved, select a trader to copy, and the software will then buy and sell with your money in exact proportion to the copied trader's funds.

Traders you can copy are generally called 'signal providers'. That is because their trading accounts send out a signal every time they make a move in the markets. You can usually browse performance stats and rating on signal providers to help you choose who to copy. Often you can spread your risk and copy many traders at the same time.

Two big companies that specialise in copy trading are ZuluTrade and DupliTrade. Many brokers offer access to their systems. In practice, you will have to sign up with a copy trade provider as well as with a partner broker. A further option is MQL5, who offer a subscription model whereby you pay signal providers to copy their trades. Getting the tech co-ordinated for this kind of deal can be a little daunting, but plenty of investors manage it.

What is a lot easier for the beginner investor is to sign up with eToro, who offer their own CopyTrader service. This is easy and free to use. Another newbie option is Avasocial, which is a mobile-only copy trading app run by big brokerage AvaTrade.

Copy trading: benefits and risks

Benefits	Risks
✓ Save time by investing without ever having to check market prices.	✦ Easy to get deceived by figures which show a signal provider has achieved dramatic growth, but do not stress that this has been achieved by taking big risks.

Benefits	Risks
✓ Copying multiple signal providers at the same time allows you to diversify and spread risk.	✦ How well a signal provider has done in the past is no guarantee that they will replicate their success in the future.
✓ Learn as you go from traders with far more experience than yourself.	✦ Newbies can lose money fast if they do not understand how to set up their risk management preferences properly: stop loss is your friend!

What should I look for in brokers that provide copy trading?

☑ **Regulation**

Make sure the company is regulated. If a broker is regulated, you are more likely to hang onto your money in the event of it going bust.

☑ **Large amount of users**

The more people already using a broker, the more reliable it is likely to be.

☑ **Good choice of signal providers**

The more signal providers you can choose from to

copy, the more chance you have of spreading risk. Note that the unregulated company MQL5 offers thousands of signal providers, as does ZuluTrade. But DupliTrade offers less than twenty.

☑ **Vetted signal providers**
DupliTrade is one of the few copy trading providers that thoroughly vets and audits their signal providers. With eToro, for example, the idea is rather that figures speak for themselves: with all sorts of stats and charts, you can see how a provider's portfolio has performed, and make a decision based on that.

WHAT ASSETS CAN I INVEST IN?

'Assets put money in your pocket, whether you work or not, and liabilities take money from your pocket.'

(Author Robert Kiyosaki)

Stocks
Medium Risk

Owning stock means owning a share in a company. Shares in stock are traded via stockbrokers on stock markets. The first stock exchange was the Amsterdam Stock Exchange (AEX) which opened in 1602. Since then, over 60 stock exchanges have emerged globally.

Shares in stock are available in any risk profile: low/medium/high:

Low risk stocks are blue chip stocks. These are shares in well-established companies that offer goods with a proven customer base. An example of an entire stock sector which is low risk is utilities.

Medium risk stocks can be companies which well-established but not doing so well right now, or companies with problems with a lot of potential. A medium risk sector is telecommunications: here there is a proven need for the products available, but there is also the chance that technological innovation from one quarter could turn the market on its head.

High risk stocks are those in sectors like biotech where technological development can make or break company fortunes overnight. Small cap stocks are also very risky. 'Small cap' means 'small capitalisation' which means that the total value of the company is small. Smaller companies have great growth potential. But they also have great bankruptcy potential!

Bonds
Low risk

The three most important things to grasp about bonds are that:

i) Bonds are not stocks.

ii) When stocks go down in value, bond values tend to go up. (Hence a diversified, medium-risk portfolio generally contains a mix of stocks and bonds.)

iii) When interest rates go up, bond values go down. And vice versa.

A bond is a loan agreement where you, the investor, lends money to the bond issuer for a fixed period of time. Bonds are generally issued by sovereign governments as well as corporations and are classified as a fixed income instrument. That means you can expect interest payments coming in from the bond issuer whilst you own the bond. These interest rates are called 'coupon payments' and are set at a 'coupon rate' specific to the bond. You can sell a bond up until the point when it reaches its 'maturity date'. At maturity date, the bond issuer will pay you back what you paid for the bond in the first place.

A key determinant of a bond's value is the credit rating of its issuer. With a US Treasury bond, for example, the issuer has an exemplary credit rating. There is little chance that the US government will default on its agreement with you and fail to pay you back your investment on bond maturity.

With junk bonds, however, the issuer has a low credit rating. This has two implications. Firstly, there is a higher chance that the issuer may go bust and your bond will be worth nothing. Secondly, the 'coupon rate' of a junk bond will be much higher; you will, in other words, get a higher yield from the bond because it is more risky.

There are many types of bond, including zero-coupon bonds, convertible bonds and callable bonds. A safe way to gain exposure to bonds without knowing too much about the ins and outs of them is to invest in a bond fund.

Funds
Low risk

Mutual funds help you, the beginner investor, to benefit from the experience of professional investors as well as spread your risk around several assets at once.

A fund manager will invest in a variety of assets on behalf of fund members who then reap the benefits (or losses). Funds can be divided into active and passive funds. Active funds are managed by a real human being, and usually therefore charge higher fees. Passive funds are not managed, and usually therefore charge lower fees.

Usually funds are managed around a particular product, or sector, or risk profile.

Index Funds

Index funds track a market index. This means that, rather than picking out particular assets, the fund reflects the value of an entire market at once. This is a great way for beginner investors to spread risk.

ETFs (Exchange Traded Funds)

98% of ETFs are passive funds. They have rocketed in popularity because they are cheaper than managed funds, whilst delivering the same benefit of spreading investor risk. The global number of ETFs rose from 276 to over 7,600 between 2003 and 2020.

ETFs can work like index funds, and track a particular index. A very well-known tracker ETF is the *SPDR S&P 500 Trust ETF,* which tracks the US *S&P 500* index of the top 500 US companies. This tracker fund is one of the main benchmarks for the US equity market. It represents companies worth a total of $374bn and has returned a 10% average annual return since its inception in 1993. ETFs do not generally pay out dividends, but this one does; dividend yield for 2020 was 1.78%.

Apart from tracker funds, ETFs are also available in particular sectors and particular products (stocks, commodities, currencies, bonds, cryptocurrencies). ETFs are also, like funds, sometimes focussed on particular risk profiles.

When it comes to fees, ETFs are much cheaper than index funds. What you need to look for is the 'expense ratio' of a fund or ETF. The SPDR S&P 500 ETF offers an expense ratio of 0.095%, for example. This means that the fund will cost the investor $0.95 for every $1000 invested. Index funds, on the other hand, tend to charge expense ratios between 0.5% and 0.75%.

If you want to trade your share in an ETF, a transaction fee of $10-$20 will usually apply.

Commodities
Medium risk

Commodities are material products in the real world like oil, precious metals or foodstuffs. You can gain exposure to commodities by investing in commodity funds, or by using CFDs.

Gold is the best-known commodity. Always think about having some gold in your portfolio. Gold is considered to be a safe haven. Its price tends to go up, very slowly. And when stock markets fall, the price of gold tends to rise.

CFDs (Contracts For Difference)
Medium to high risk

CFDs allow investors to invest in products without actually owning them. You enter rather into a contract with your broker informed by changes in asset values. CFDs give investors a massive choice in what you can invest in, particularly when it comes to commodities: you can invest in oil, for example, without needing a warehouse to store barrels of oil!

The downside of CFDs is that they tend to attract high fees. Further, they offer leveraged investing, which is a dangerous trap for beginners to fall into. Leveraged investing means you can amplify your potential gains or losses at the start of your contract. You do this by choosing a gear of 2x, 5x, 10x — even 100x. The broker will then pay you, or take from you, the change in price of the underlying asset multiplied by your chosen gear. Do not leverage your trades until you have proven success in trading.

Cryptocurrencies
High Risk

The big noise in financial markets! There are now 9000 cryptos in a sector worth over $2 trillion. And what a conundrum cryptos present to the beginner investor!

There seems to be so much potential in cryptos to get rich quick. But there is so much risk of losing money.

Volatility in the crypto sector is legendary. The market cheerleader, Bitcoin (BTC) — taking up 40% of the entire sector — was worth less than $4k a coin in January 2019 but hit a price of over $50k per coin in 2021. Dogecoin, which was intended as a joke coin, multiplied n value by 5200% between January and September 2021.

Cryptos are held virtually in electronic wallets (similar to PayPal).

Cryptocurrencies are digital currencies which are associated with specific technologies. These technologies relate to financial transactions and ways of organising them in an encrypted way on the internet. A crypto is often the native form of exchange in a system that manages financial transactions in conventional currencies.

You have probably heard of Ethereum? Ethereum is software that allows users to build transaction-related software applications, and its native currency is Ether (ETH). Ether claims 20% of the entire crypto sector. Investors think Ethereum is the future of behind-the-scenes blockchain/ distributed ledger technology, so Ether is a popular crypto to invest in.

All cryptocurrencies are linked to blockchain/distributed ledger technology.

Blockchains are packets of encrypted data. They are a way of recording financial transactions in an encrypted way. This is very useful to global commerce.

Blockchain technology allows financial transactions to be done far quicker than conventional banking systems. A crypto called XRP, for example, is based on technology from a company called Ripple Labs. Their blockchain transaction technology takes 4 seconds to validate a financial transaction, whereas the conventional banking's SWIFT system takes up to four days! If you buy XRP, you are buying into the belief that Ripple's technology is a winner.

So, unlike conventional companies, cryptocurrencies do not make money. When you invest in a crypto, you are investing in a particular form of money that may prove very popular in the future. This is why some established investors think cryptos are a bubble market, which will eventually collapse. Of crypto-trading, Berkshire Hathaway Vice Chairman Charlie Munger famously remarked: *'it's like everybody else is trading turds and you decide you can't be left out.'*

$140bn in cryptos has been lost to people forgetting their password to their crypto wallet.

An average of $10m gets stolen from crypto exchanges every day.

And yet, 85 out of 100 European and US institutional investors polled in January 2021 said they were planning to begin investing in cryptos, or increase their existing crypto holding. That's because cryptos are thought to be a great hedge against inflation in other currencies. Most cryptos have an upper limit on the amount that can be in circulation, so their price cannot fall, as with conventional currencies, because of over-supply.

If you are going to invest in cryptos, keep your investment to 1% and 5% of your total stock market funds. It is only natural that you want to get in on rocketing prices. But the sector is very new and dangerous for beginners.

WHICH INVESTMENT STRATEGY SHOULD I CHOOSE?

'The essence of strategy is choosing what not to do.'

(Economist Michael E. Porter)

Let's get this out of the way...

Forget about day trading

Investing is not gambling. As a new investor, do not therefore be tempted to head straight into day trading.

Day trading is when you try and take advantage of short-term gains and losses in asset prices: you might open and close several positions in one day.

The foreign exchange markets (forex) are popular with day traders who effectively bet on the difference in movements between pairs of currencies. Day trading in commodities as well as cryptocurrencies is also popular. But you really have to know what you are doing. Without expert knowledge and/or some fancy computer algorithms, you will lose your money.

Investing is about putting money away for the long-term. This allows the money to do the work for you. Despite the occasional bad year, stock markets rise gradually year by year. You can deploy various strategies to optimise your growth in capital in the financial markets. But you must get into the habit of taking the long-term view —at least until you have some experience under your belt.

Forget about leveraged trading

Leveraged trading is when you gear up your gains and losses. You can do this with CFDs (Contracts for Difference). It can be tempting: you are certain that an asset is going to rise in value, so you decide to maximise what you can gain. But you are not a fortune-teller. The asset can fall in value too. And, if it does, you will have maximised your losses.

Leveraging is often offered in ratios of 2x, 5x, 10x.

Example:

Stock A is available at $1. You decide to buy 100 Stock As at a gearing of 2x. You do not pay any more for a leveraged trade usually: the cost of 100 Stock As will still be $100, whether you leverage or not.

The price of Stock A then rises to $1.10. Because you are leveraged at 2x, you will gain 2x the gain in stock price. So, instead of gaining $0.10 for every Stock A you own, you will gain 2x $0.10 = $0.20. Great, right? But not if Stock A fails in price by $0.10 to $0.90 per share. Because then you will lose $0.20 for every Stock A you own.

How do I invest for sustained cashflow?

Cashflow? If you want to invest for cashflow, your best bet is to invest in property. Then you can expect regular inflow of cash via rents. This is, by far, the best proven investment route for achieving regular sums of cash coming in.

Invest in REITs

REITs are Real Estate Investment Trusts. These allow you to gain exposure to property values without actually buying or selling property.

The great thing about REITs, which are run by corporations, is that 90% of profits must be paid out in dividends. This means you can be sure of a regular annual income from your investment.

Invest in dividend-paying companies

On the stock market, your best bet for sustained cashflow is to invest in particular stocks that pay high dividends. A dividend is an annual payment to all shareholders in a company.

A guru who favours this strategy is John Robinson, founder of Nest Egg Guru in Hawaii, US.

Not many companies pay out high dividends. It is up to the company if, and when, they do so.

The stat you are looking for to find companies that pay dividends is called 'dividend payout ratio.' This describes the percentage of net income coming into a firm that goes out to investors in the form of dividends.

The advantage of holding stocks in companies that do pay dividends is that you will receive dividends as well as gain from any rise in the underlying value of the stocks.

One disadvantage of a dividend-based investment strategy is that some companies with a good reputation for paying dividends are not great when it comes to rising share values; so you might get an annual payment, but the value of the underlying stock does not move much. A further disadvantage is that you can never be sure whether a company will decide to pay out dividends or not.

A good place to start with dividend-paying companies is to have a look at the Dividend Aristocrats Index. This is run by S&P Indices. Like all indexes, it means you can invest in a range of companies as part of a big pool of people and institutions doing so too. The Dividend Aristocrats Index allows you to invest in several companies at once that have paid increasing dividends for 25 consecutive years.

WHAT IS A DIVIDEND?

A dividend is an annual payment made by a company to all holders of shares in that company. That could include you! (if you have bought shares in the company). Companies can choose whether to pay a dividend or not. Some never do, some do every year.

Invest in bonds

Bonds are a fixed-income investment. They are low-risk — because they are issued by sovereign governments and established corporations — and therefore do not offer stellar returns. The chances of you losing your money are small, unless you invest in what are known as 'junk bonds'.

You might buy a treasury of corporate bond for $1000. This means effectively you are lending the issuer $1000. After a fixed term of years, the issuer will pay you back your principal (ie. your $1000). In the meantime they will pay you interest payments, called 'coupon payments'.

Rather than investing in bonds directly, you can invest in bond funds. This means a professional will invest in a number of different bonds on your behalf and you will receive regular payments. The downside is that you will likely have to pay management fees to the company managing the bond fund.

Other strategies for sustainable income

Another option would be to save up the start-up costs for your own business and aim, eventually, to pay yourself a salary. With most start-ups, though, you will be unlikely to be able to pay yourself for quite a while.

Another proven technique is to invest in a pension. A pension is a financial product that allows your money to build up over the years, accrue interest – and then come back to you in regular payments, or even lump sum amounts.

Pensions can be complicated. And they are boring. But what's wrong with boring? Boring is good in investing, because it means you are not losing money. Boring means you are letting time do the work for you.

I have a high risk appetite. What investment strategies are right for me?

If you are a beginner investor and have a high risk appetite, there is a special club you can join.

It is called the 'broke' club!

You may need to make money fast. And you may have decided that the stock market is the place to do it. If this is the case, start small and follow one simple rule:

Do not invest money you cannot afford to lose.

If you can follow that rule, consider a second one:

Stick to your investment plan.

What leads high-risk investors to lose their money is to chop and change their strategy. This is understandable in the heat of the moment.

If you are looking to make money fast, then what you really need to be doing is trading, rather than investing.

Trading means buying and selling assets. Day trading, as we have mentioned, involves doing this several times a day. Forex (foreign exchange) is a popular market in which to day trade, and it is a seductive business.

HOW DOES FOREX WORK?

Forex (foreign exchange) works by betting on the price difference between pairs of currencies. This price difference is called the spread. The spread is measured in 'pips'. Three formats exist defined by risk. Low risk: 'major pairs' twin two major currencies with low volatility. Medium risk: 'minor pairs' match one major currency with another currency with higher volatility. 'Exotics' match two minor currencies with high volatility.

That's because you can get lucky in forex many times without knowing what you are doing. The problem is that you might then be tempted to trade in greater amounts, and even risk leveraged trading.

If you are determined to follow a high-risk investment strategy, consider:

☑ **Cryptocurrencies**

Some people say cryptos are the future of all financial transactions. And others say they are literally worthless because they do not generate money in their own right. Either way, the crypto sector is the wild west of investing. Volatility is off the scale. Prices across the whole sector sometimes go and up down 10%+ in a day. Your best strategy? Either get in a crypto that is surging upwards and be ready to sell at a moment's notice. This is a terrible form of investing, and almost bound to fail – but sometimes you might get super-lucky. Or do your research, make a decision which crypto is going to be used widely in the future, and buy for the long-term. You will have to weather some scary times probably. But if you want high-risk investing, here it is.

☑ **ICOs**

An ICO (International Coin Offering) marks the debut of a crypto onto the market. If you have done your research, you may have good reason to invest at the beginning of a crypto's journey. But it can all go terribly wrong if the market is not interested, and the price of the crypto goes into a nosedive shortly after launch.

☑ **IPOs**

Investing in an Initial Public Offering means buying shares that are coming to market for the first time from an established conventional company. An IPO is, in theory, a good place to get in at the bottom of the price ladder. But the problem with IPOs is that they are unpredictable. Market sentiment can swing, and even an established company that has good financial fundamentals and a good business record can be snubbed by the market, resulting in its share price falling off rapidly. Taxi and tech firm Uber, for example, suffered a terrible IPO. A key problem for beginners with IPOs is that a lot of media hype usually surrounds them, and it is difficult to see what the real story is.

☑ **Venture capital**

This means investing in start-ups. You may be able to do this direct. Or you may be able to find a fund that invests in start-ups. Either way, the risks are sky-high because the companies which require your investment of venture capital could just quickly fold. The potential gain is sky-high too, because the company could go on to be the next Apple. One big problem with venture capital for beginners is that a high minimum investment is usually asked for.

☑ **Emerging markets**

Across the world, underdeveloped countries are waking up economically. If you time it right, you can get in on periods of incredible growth. For example, China was a great country to invest in between 2010 and 2018. The best way to invest in emerging markets is to find an ETF (Exchange Traded Fund) that specialises in them.

☑ **High yield bonds**

High yield bonds are often called junk bonds. You can guess why! Junk bonds are issued by companies that have been given low credit ratings. As a result, they have to offer higher coupon rates (interest) on the money you lend them by buying their bond. If the company does not go bust, a junk bond is therefore great, because you receive high yields. If the company does go bust, you get no payments and you won't be able to sell the bond. You can spread your risk here by investing in a bond fund that specialises in high yield bonds.

✦ Ignore day trading, currency trading and options. For a beginner, even one determined to risk everything, these present the quickest route to financial ruin.

I have a medium risk appetite. What investment strategies are right for me?

The great thing about a medium risk appetite is that you can include high risk elements in your strategy. A medium risk appetite means you will not lose out on exciting opportunities. But, to ensure you do not go broke, you will also balance the potential big winners with low risk investments that offer less exciting rewards.

The bad thing about a medium risk profile is that you are unlikely to make much money in weeks. You need to be thinking in terms of six-month intervals. Ideally, you need to be prepared to hold onto shares for years. Investment guru Philip Fisher famously held Motorola stock between 1955 and his death in 2004.

The best strategy for medium risk investing is to develop a diversified portfolio.

DIVERSIFIED PORTFOLIO

This means having a selection of different financial assets in your portfolio. The aim is to spread risk, so if there is a crash in one area, the value of your portfolio will only take a dent, rather than collapse completely. Don't keep your eggs in one basket!

What is the basic balance of a diversified portfolio?

Begin with a simple division of 60% stock exposure and 40% bonds. 'Stock exposure' means being exposed to the stock market which you can do outside of pure stocks via mutual funds and ETFs.

Why are stocks and bonds balanced in this way in a diversified portfolio? Because when stocks go down in value, bonds tend to rise in value. That's because they are perceived as a safe haven, therefore become more popular, and their prices thus rise.

If you want a more conservative diversified portfolio, switch the percentages and go for 40% stock exposure and 60% bonds. Remember that you can always stiffen up your risk management by investing in funds (like ETFs) which invest in entire markets (via indices) or many stocks or bonds at the same time. Funds spread risk. ETFs in particular have become very popular because they offer low costs compared to traditional mutual funds, and spread risk very well. An ETF that tracks the index of an entire stock market, such as the SPDR S&P 500 Trust ETF, is an excellent addition to any diversified portfolio.

What other assets should I buy for my diversified portfolio?

To keep your portfolio balanced, consider adding one higher risk asset at the same time as you add one lower risk asset.

So, for example, if you fancy dedicating 1-5% of your portfolio to high-risk cryptocurrencies, ensure you also dedicate 1-5% with a low risk asset. Gold is great low risk commodity. Gold rarely takes off in value, but its price has risen over fourfold since the financial crisis of 2007-2008. Investors tend to buy gold when the stock market is in trouble, because it is considered a safe haven: gold is a commodity that people will always want to buy.

I have a low risk appetite. What investment strategies are right for me?

In the financial markets, a combination of index funds, blue chip stocks and bonds would be considered a good basis for a diversified low risk portfolio.

Outside the financial markets, for low-risk investments look to retail products from banks.

A good example of a low-risk financial product is an annuity. Annuities are often used as a pension product for retirement planning. This an arrangement whereby you pay a lump sum upfront in return for a series of payments over time.

If you hang in there, and the issuing company does not go bust, you will end up with more money than you invested. The problem with annuities is that the interest rates you receive are not impressive. You might find you barely keep pace with inflation, although an annuities salesman would probably beg to differ!

One of the lowest risk financial investment products is a high interest savings account with a retail bank. Do not rule this out if you really cannot afford to lose money. But, again, ensure that the interest rates offered are higher than the rate of inflation — or your money will sit there actually losing value over the years.

How should I choose which stocks are right for me?

Generally, you want to be looking for stocks that will go up in value.

You can, instead, look for stocks that you think will drop in value and 'go short' on them. This means buying them in a particular arrangement with your broker that means you will gain as they drop. This can be a good technique for a bear market — when prices are dropping generally — but only if you are trading for the short term. And trading for the short term is not the best way for a beginner to build wealth over the long term.

STOCK PICKING

Stock picking means choosing the right stocks for your portfolio. There are many techniques used to do this: and hearing about a 'hot stock' in the media is the least reliable! Remember that if, as a beginner, you get to hear of a hot prospect, its value has probably already been priced into the market. If you are going to invest on the basis of media news, do so with money you can afford to lose.

How do I pick stocks that will rise in value?

- ☑ Copy knowledgeable investors automatically by using a broker that offers copy trading.

- ☑ Do some research according on what expert investors look for, and then start digging through stock statistics yourself.

As a starting point, consider this piece of advice from investment guru Warren Buffett. He said: *'it's far better to buy a wonderful company at a fair price than a fair company at a wonderful price.'*

That's because the chances of a fair company taking off in value are small, whereas a wonderful company is more likely to soar at some point in the future. A further moral of Buffett's quote here is: take the time to find the real gems. Don't bother yourself with companies that are 'kind of OK'. Because they will likely only ever do 'kind of OK.'

Buffett also advised that, if you don't feel comfortable owning a stock for 10 years, you shouldn't own it for 10 minutes. That's bad news for those of us who need to make big money right now! But the point he is making is to stay disciplined.

If you set yourself in to hold stocks for a long time, you will not panic and sell them at exactly the wrong moment. If an investor lets emotion them, they are likely to sell at the bottom or start buying at the peak; either way, your portfolio will collapse if you keep doing this.

☑ Buffett got a lot of his thinking from his mentor, Benjamin Graham. He wrote a famous book called *The Intelligent Investor*. This introduces the idea of 'value investing', which is to find companies that are performing well as well as going for a relatively cheap price compared to the revenues they are likely to bring in over future years.

☑ Another expert in long-term growth is Philip Fisher, a professional investor often dubbed the 'father of growth stocks'. From the 1930s to the end of the century, Fisher ran a highly-successful investment company called Fisher & Company. He wrote a classic book called *Common Stocks and Uncommon Profits.*

If we are looking for stocks that are likely to rise in value over the long-term, Fisher said we should look at two aspects of a company: its management, and the business itself.

In its management, we should be looking for:

☑ Robust personnel policies.

☑ Good financial controls.

☑ Leaders who are happy with, but not fixated on, change.

☑ Integrity.

☑ Conservative accounting.

In a firm's business characteristics, we should look for:

- ☑ A range of their own products/services.

- ☑ A leading industry position.

- ☑ Good sales department.

- ☑ Committed research and development.

- ☑ High profit margins.

- ☑ Growth outlook.

These are the sort of details you can winkle out of the internet by putting a company's name in the search bar. Some characteristics you will be able to get immediately from the company's own website. But others you will need to find out from other sources.

Open a simple file on your prospect, whether on your computer or on paper, and start to build up a picture of its strengths and weaknesses. Be patient. And don't just invest in a company because you have spent a long time researching it!

Another investment guru with some stock picking tips to share is Peter Lynch. Over just 13 years, he grew the

Fidelity Magellan Fund from $20m to $14bn. In 11 of these 13 years, Lynch's portfolio outperformed the *S&P 500* Index by achieving an annual average return of 29%.

Lynch famously had 8 rules which he applied to every stock picking process:

1. 'Know what you know'.

2. Don't try and predict what the economy/interest rates are going to do next.

3. Steer clear of long shots.

4. If a business has good management, it is a good business.

5. Be humble. Admit to your mistakes, and learn from them.

6. Before you buy anything, you should be able to explain to anybody exactly why this is the right stock.

7. There is always something to worry about with your portfolio; make sure you know what it is!

8. Don't rush. You have plenty of time to find companies that are exceptional. (If they are exceptional, they won't be going anywhere).

What has 'financial analysis' got to do with picking stocks?

Financial analysis is when you look at certain stats about a company in the hope that they show whether the company is worth investing in.

This is what we call looking at the 'fundamentals' of a company. This is 'quantitative analysis'.

Qualitative analysis, on the other hand, is when you look at features of the company like its approach to business (business model), its management, its governance, and its competition.

If you brush up your accountancy skills (!), you can look at company balance sheets, income statements, and statements of cash flows. Of these, statements of cash flows are the least confusing, and the least easy for accountants to hide bad news in. A company has either got cash going through its books or not. Certainly, learning how to read a company balance sheet is a great skill to develop, but you can get a broad-brush overview of a company by getting to grips with a few simple stats which are usually available:

Debt/Equity ratio

This stat should give you a good broad indication of a company's financial health. Debt/Equity ratio describes the proportion of a company's debt to its assets. It is like describing the proportion between somebody's outstanding mortgage, and the amount of the house they currently own. Note that some sectors have far higher debt/equity ratios than others. If a company has a high debt/equity ratio, it means it is in a lot of debt.

P/E Ratio

This ratio is a good way to compare companies in different sectors.

The P/E ratio for a company is usually easily accessible by an internet search. If not, you can arrive at the P/E ratio by dividing the company's share price by the value for its annual earnings per share (EPS).

If a firm has a higher P/E ratio than its competitors, it means investors are prepared to pay more to get in on its earnings.

On the one hand, a high P/E ratio may indicate that the company is going to take off. On the other hand, a high P/E ratio may indicate that the company is overvalued.

Certainly a low P/E ratio means that the share price is low compared to its earnings, which might suggest it is undervalued. Remember that undervalued stocks do not, unfortunately, always rise in value.

Price/Sales Ratio

This ratio is a good one to find if you are getting bamboozled by too many stats. That's because it involves actual sales figures. A company with a low price/sales ratio is potentially a bargain. That's because, the lower the ratio, investors are paying a lower price to get a share in more sales.

Profit margin

This is the amount of profit a firm reaps for every unit of product or service that it sells. This can be a misleading stat. Ideally, you want a company that has high profit margins. That's because the company has found a way of selling goods with a good profit. A low profit margin, on the other hand, could indicate the company is inefficient, because it spends too much creating its offering to market. But profit margins differ wildly between sectors, so it can be confusing. The software industry, for example, has big profit margins. But in groceries, profit margins tend to be very low.

EBITDA

EBITDA is term you will hear a lot. It means Earnings Before Interest Taxes, Depreciation and Amortisation. It shows, cleanly, how much money is coming in. An EBITDA of over 10 is considered good.

EBITDA/sales ratio (also known as EBITDA margin)

This stat shows you how profitable a company is by comparing gross income to sales. The EBITDA margin shows you how much income the firm actually gets for each dollar of sales revenue. You want this ratio to be as high as possible.

A high EBITDA margin (60%) shows that a company is keeping its costs low and selling efficiently.

What is technical charting?

'Chartists' say technical charting is a science. Others say it is nonsense! It can certainly be very absorbing.

Technical charting is when you analyse graphs of a company's stock over time, and look for distinctive patterns. These patterns are held by some to indicate what the stock price is going to do next.

Sometimes, technical charting works. Sometimes, it does not (but the same can be said of analysing the fundamentals of a company with financial analysis).

Chartists divide their analysis into continuation patterns and reversal patterns.

Continuation patterns do not, as you would assume, indicate necessarily that a stock price will continue in the same direction. They indicate rather a break in a trend, which could then go either way. Pennants, flags and wedges are examples of continuation patterns.

Reversal patterns, on the other hand, are held to indicate that a stock price is likely to change direction. Head and shoulder, double top and double bottom are examples of reversal patterns.

HOW DO I CHOOSE AN ONLINE BROKER?

'It is choice – not chance – that determines your destiny.'

(Entrepreneur Jean Nidetch)

What should I look for in an online broker?

The first big thing to look for is whether a broker will accept you as a client depending on the region you live in. Etoro, for example, has 20m clients in 100 countries around the world. TD Ameritrade, as well as other big US brokers, only accept clients from the US.

A second important thing is whether your broker will take your native currency. Some brokers allow you to deposit funds in currencies other than their main currency (USD, GBP or EUR, depending on location).

But, if your native currency differs from the main currency in use with your broker, you will have to pay a currency conversion fee. This fee will apply when you pay in funds and when you withdraw them too.

The third big thing you should look for is regulation. Regulation means that a national government has an eye on the broker. A regulated broker has all the right paperwork. If you use a broker that is not regulated, you will not be protected if the broker is over-charging or if it goes bust.

Other key things to look for in an online broker include:

☑ Availability of learning materials and demo account.

☑ Range of financial products available to invest in.

☑ Fees, commissions, and spreads (the difference between buying and selling prices).

What fees do online brokers charge?

Commissions

Some brokers charge commissions per transaction. That means when you buy or sell an asset, they will hit you with a fixed fee. Commissions sometimes work such that you will be charged per unit of financial asset: so if you buy 100 shares, a small commission will apply to each of the 100 shares, rather than apply to the transaction as a whole. Sometimes, both a transaction and proportional fee will apply at the same time.

Commissions are less common than they used to be. They tend to be particularly common with CFD (Contracts For Difference) transactions and in obscure markets.

Get your calculator out before you buy or sell!

Spreads

A spread is not a fee or commission, but rather a way that brokers make money. Spreads are an important concept that you must understand.

The spread describes the difference between the price at which a broker is prepared to buy an asset and the price at which they are prepared to sell an asset.

A spread is often called the 'bid/ask' spread, which means buy/sell' spread.

Suppose Stock A is listed as being worth $100. An online broker might sell it to you for $100. They might also be prepared to buy it from you for $100. In this case, there is no spread.

A broker that does use spreads may be prepared to buy Stock A at $90 (thus making $10 on the deal) and sell it only at $110 (thus making $10 on the deal).

In this example, the spread is used by the broker is $20. That means the stock price has to move $20 for you to make any money, whether you are buying 'long' in the hope that the price will rise, or going 'short' in the hope that it will fall. Either way, you must remember about spreads, or you can get caught out and lose profit.

If Stock A rises in value, for example, by $5 to hit $105, you might think you have made $5 for every Stock A that you own. But the spread will follow the rise in price. That means the broker, given the new list price of $105, will only buy Stock A at $95 and sell at $115. Given that you paid $110 for each Stock A, you will then actually lose $15 for each Stock A that you sell.

The spread example here is many times larger than those you will encounter in real life. But watch out for spreads! They tend to be heavy for cryptocurrencies, for example.

Overnight fees

Overnight fees apply to short-term trades in CFDs when you want to hold a position overnight.

Withdrawal fees

Every time you withdraw funds, you may be charged a withdrawal fee. eToro, for example, levies a flat fee of $5 per withdrawal.

What happens if my online broker goes bust?

There is a chance that another broker will step in and buy the business. Then your account will be safe and simply be registered with the new purchaser. Otherwise, if the broker is regulated, there is a chance that a sovereign government will step in. In this case, depending on the regulating country, some or all of your funds and assets will remain safe.

5 top online brokers for beginners

You are going to have to do your own research to track down the perfect broker for you. A lot depends on what assets you want to trade in. But what it all boils down to is which country you live in. You can ask around on the internet to find brokers which serve your particular country of residence.

And do not be discouraged. The online brokerage market is fast-growing. Brokers are bringing out new services and extending their scope all the time.

Below are 5 brokers to review as a starting point.

We have no affiliation with any of the brokers mentioned. So it is from a completely independent perspective that we would recommend eToro as your first port of call. With 20m customers in a 100 countries, eToro have invested heavily in making their online brokerage easy to use with plenty of learning materials and investment options that develop all the time.

If you are a US citizen, then TD Ameritrade offer a good experience for beginners. In the US, other excellent broker sites are provided by Charles Schwab, Vanguard and Fidelity.

For European traders, the market is not as well developed as in the UK and US. Consider eToro, but also look at Degiro which offers good access to European citizens and is developing a good name for itself.

eToro

Best for:	Beginner investors
Website	Etoro.com
Accepts clients from:	100+ countries: a truly global brokerage
Trading on mobile phone?:	Yes
Tradeable assets:	Stocks, commodities, funds, ETFs, CFDs, cryptocurrencies, forex (depending on your country)
Minimum deposit:	50 USD (or equivalent)
Deposit options	Bank transfer, credit cards and many electronic wallets including PayPal
What currency can I use to make a deposit?:	USD, EUR, GBP and others – but currency conversion fees apply for all but USD

Best for:	Beginner investors
Fees:	No commission charged on equity trades Commission charged on CFDs Withdrawal fee (5 USD) Big (expensive) spreads on cryptocurrencies
Regulated:	FCA in UK, CySec for use in Europe, and elsewhere
Benefits:	Big social community and copy trading available Huge investment in making it easy to use Great range of assets to invest in
Disadvantages:	✦ Choice of options can be confusing ✦ Wide range of fees depending on asset traded

TD Ameritrade

Best for:	Beginners based in the US
Website:	www.tdameritrade.com
Accepts clients from:	US
Trading on mobile phone?:	Yes
Tradeable assets:	Stocks, options, ETFs, funds, futures, forex; some cryptocurrency capability via *ErisX*
Minimum deposit:	$0
Deposit options	Bank transfer only – no credit cards or electronic wallets
What currency can I use to make a deposit?:	USD – you need to be a US citizen to join
Fees:	High fees for trading in funds, but low trading fees otherwise Free trading on stocks and ETFs
Regulated:	US Securities and Exchange Commission, and others

Best for:	Beginners based in the US
Benefits:	Free stock and ETF trading Great platform to use Great customer support as well as learning tools
Disadvantages:	✦ You can only trade on US markets ✦ Need to be a US resident ✦ No credit card/electronic wallet deposit

Degiro

Best for:	European investors
Website	www.degiro.com
Accepts clients from:	Europe and UK
Trading on mobile phone?:	Yes
Tradeable assets:	Stocks, ETFs, funds, bonds, options, futures
Minimum deposit:	$0
Deposit options	Bank transfer only – no credit cards or electronic wallets
What currency can I use to make a deposit?:	USD, GBP, EUR
Fees:	Proportional fee per share traded + small fixed fee No withdrawal fee
Regulated:	FCA in the UK and BaFin in Germany

Best for:	European investors
Benefits:	Simple to use Cheap fees Good European coverage
Disadvantages:	✦ You can't trade in cryptos, CFDs or forex ✦ Limited research tools ✦ Deposit only with bank transfer

Revolut

Best for:	Slimline, easy investing
Website:	Revolut.com
Accepts clients from:	Europe, Australia, Canada, Singapore, Switzerland, US
Trading on mobile phone?:	Yes
Tradeable assets:	800 US stocks, gold, silver and some cryptocurrencies
Minimum deposit:	$0
Deposit options:	Bank transfer only
What currency can I use to make a deposit?:	Many, but currency conversion fee applies to all deposit currencies other than USD
Fees:	Free stock trading for UK stocks Other fees apply
Regulated:	SEC in the US, FCA in the UK

Best for:	Slimline, easy investing
Benefits:	Easy and fast to open account Free stock trading User-friendly
Disadvantages:	✦ No 2-step login ✦ No learning materials or demo account ✦ Limited range of assets to invest in

Interactive Brokers

Best for:	Wide range of investment options
Website:	www.interactivebrokers.com
Accepts clients from:	Around the globe, including Europe, US, UK, China
Trading on mobile phone?:	Yes
Tradeable assets:	Stocks, ETFs, forex, funds, bonds, options, futures, CFDs and cryptocurrencies
Minimum deposit:	$100
Deposit options	Bank transfer only
What currency can I use to make a deposit?:	Several account base currencies offered. Other than these currencies, a conversion fee will apply
Fees:	Commissions charged on trades First withdrawal per month is free

Best for:	Wide range of investment options
Regulated:	SEC in the USA, FCA in the UK
Benefits:	Wide range of investment assets Great global user reach Low fees
Disadvantages:	✦ Complicated account opening process ✦ Interface not great for beginners ✦ Limited customer service

Is there an alternative to using an online broker?

Yes.

If you have millions, you can instruct a bank to appoint a portfolio manager to do your investing for you.

If you have tens of thousands, you can appoint an Independent Financial Advisor (IFA), and they will invest for you. For the rest of us, online brokers are the place to make our investments.

Independent Financial Advisors (IFAs) – Advantages and Disadvantages

IFAs generally work alone. But usually they are attached to a company that has secured a license for a group of IFAs to work legally.

Benefits	Disadvantages
IFAs are trained to review your whole financial situation and deliver solutions. That means advising on retail financial products as well as investment in the financial markets.	✦ IFAs usually charge a management fee, and a succession of fees on investments that you make.

Benefits	Disadvantages
Even if they are relatively new to their career, IFAs are trained, full-time professionals. They will be able to review your financial situation and immediately suggest a host of possible options that you would otherwise have to research.	✦ If the markets move the wrong way, you cannot sue your IFA. It is not their fault if your holdings drop in value, and they cannot predict the future any more than you can.
A key advantage offered by IFAs is objectivity. The better they advise you, the better their reputation. So they are good allies. But what makes them great allies is that they are not emotionally linked to your financial fortunes. This means they can give sober advice when your own head may be full of emotion.	✦ Only experience will tell whether you land yourself with a duff advisor. There are still some in the global sector who are not up to scratch.

How should I recruit an IFA?

Providing financial advice is an area that has attracted some shady players in the past. Integrity, communication, experience, regulation and expertise are what you are looking for. Be sure you get hold of an IFA you can trust by asking them the following questions prior to engagement:

- ☑ Can you provide testimonials?

- ☑ What qualifications do you have?

- ☑ Who are you (and your company) regulated by?

- ☑ Do you charge fees, earn commission, or both?

- ☑ How regularly will you review my portfolio?

- ☑ Can I contact you direct in the event of a financial emergency?

- ☑ How often will you personally contact me?

INVESTMENT JARGON – EXPLAINED

'I think we invent jargon because it saves time talking to one-another'

(Mathematician John Maynard Smith)

Bears

Bears are people who say that the markets are heading downhill in value. A 'bear' market is one, therefore, in which prices are dropping.

Blue chip stock

A blue chip stock is a heavyweight company with a solid reputation. Google, Coca Cola, and Apple are examples of blue chip stocks.

The advantage of investing in blue chip stocks is that they are unlikely to go bust or suddenly drop in value — but that does not mean they cannot. Both Enron and Volkswagen were judged to be blue chip stocks before scandals decimated their share price.

The disadvantage of blue chip stocks is that they are unlikely to make dramatic gains in price. But they may grow steadily over time.

Bulls

Bulls are people who say that the markets are heading higher. A 'bull' market is one, therefore, in which prices are rising.

CFDs

Contracts For Difference. CFDs allow you to buy into assets without actually owning the underlying asset. With a CFD, you can buy into a commodity like oil, for example, without owning barrels of oil. CFDs offer leveraged trading, which can get you into trouble. CFDs are currently banned in the US.

Double bottom, double top

'Double bottom' and 'double top' are technical charting terms.

A 'double bottom' is when the share price hits a new low, rises a little, then hits the same low again. The price bottoms out. Often, the price will then rise. That's because the price has reached the point at which people see the stock as good value again.

A 'double top' is when a share price hits a new high, drops a little, then hits the same high again. The prices tops out. Often, the price will then drop. That's because the price has reached the point at which people see the stock as over-valued.

Equity

Stocks and shares.

Fundamentals

If you are taking the sensible decision to invest for the long-haul, 'fundamentals' are your friend.

'Fundamentals' describe the financial metrics of a company like sales figures, EBITDA and P/E ratio. If the fundamentals of a company are good, it means the company is well-run and likely to make good money in the future.

GBP, USD, EUR

These are how certain key currencies are notated. GBP stands for Great British Pound. USD stands for United States Dollar. EUR stands for Euro.

Going long/going short

'Going long' means buying normally, in the hope that the asset will rise in value and you can sell it at a profit.

'Going short' means buying into a stock with a particular arrangement whereby you make money when the asset falls in value. This is often called 'shorting a stock'. Most brokers provide this service for stocks. It means you can still make money even if the markets are falling in value.

Priced into the market

Suppose a company is doing a big product launch, and the word is that the launch will go well ...

... You might think it would be a good idea to buy stocks now, right?

The problem is that this good news of the product launch is likely to be 'priced into the market'. This means, as soon as a few people get to know of the likely success of the product launch, the price of the stock goes up. For the beginner, it is now usually too late to benefit by buying in.

EBITDA

EBITDA stands for 'Earnings Before Interest, Taxes, Depreciation and Amortisation'. It shows how much gross income the company boasts.

('Amortisation', by the way, can mean two things. If you amortise an asset, it means putting a financial figure to it for accounting purposes. If you amortise a debt, it means paying it off over a period of time.)

MT4/MT5

Stands for 'MetaTrader 4/MetaTrader 5'. These are free trading platforms used by pros that some brokers give access to. Not for newbies!

P/E ratio

'Price-to-Earnings' ratio. This is a popular way of valuing a company. The term describes the ratio of the price of a share in a company divided by the company's figure for earnings per share (EPS). Firms with high P/E ratios are expensive. Firms with low P/E ratios are cheap.

Spreads

A 'spread' describes the difference between the price at which you can buy an asset with a broker, and a price at which you can sell it. Often referred to as a 'bid/ask spread.' You want as low a spread as possible. Otherwise, when the price moves, some or all of your potential profit will be lost in the spread.

Example of a spread: stock A is priced at $100. A broker might offer a spread of $95-$105. This means you can buy stock A for $105 (giving the broker $5) or sell Stock A for $95 (giving the broker $5). Spreads are one way by which brokers make money.

Stop Loss

Stop losses can save you from disaster! Putting a 'stop loss' on a trade means that, if the price of an asset falls below a certain level, your online broker's software will automatically sell the asset. This stops you losing too much money in the event of an asset's price going into freefall.

Technical trading/charting

'Technical charting' is when you analyse charts of stock prices over time, looking for patterns. These patterns are often indicators of price movements to come.

The problem is, that sometimes these technical patterns are not reliable indicators at all! Technical charting is viewed as a science by some, and nonsense by others.

An example of a technical charting term is a 'double bottom' and double top'.

Technical trading is when you invest and trade in assets on the basis of chart analysis.

Timing the market

This means buying when prices are at their lowest. Makes sense, right? But the reality is that timing the market is very difficult — even with the algorithms and resources of a major trading house. If you pursue a 'value investing' strategy, you do not need to time the market. That is because a strong company, with good fundamentals, will rise in value whatever happens. The same is true of stock markets in general. Instead of 'timing the market', buy into a market index (like the *S&P 500* Index) and hold.

Value investing

'Value investing' is famous investor Warren Buffet's strategy. This means i) finding companies that have strong 'fundamentals' and low price tags ii) buying into them and holding onto the stocks for the long-term.

Volatility

This term relates to how likely prices are to go up and down. High volatility — as we find in the cryptocurrency sector, for example — means prices change quickly and dramatically. Low volatility — as we find in the bond sector, for example — means prices change slowly and gradually.

TOP TEN TIPS FOR EFFECTIVE INVESTING

'Seeing what is not effective is effective for understanding what is effective.'

(Architect Robert Venturi)

1. Start small and build up.

2. Write your investment plan on a single page and stick to it.

3. Spread your risk with a diversified portfolio.

4. Do not invest money in high-risk assets you cannot afford to lose.

5. If you hear about a 'hot stock', chances are it is too late to gain from its rise.

6. Research stocks thoroughly.

7. Learn how to invest from investment greats, rather than trendy 'star managers'.

8.   If you try to time the market, make sure you constantly monitor prices so you can get out quickly if needed.

9.   95% of your holdings should be in 'boring' assets – that way, you will not lose everything.

10. Forget about day trading.

TOP 10 INVESTORS IN HISTORY

'An expert is a person who has made all the mistakes which can be made, in a narrow field.'

(Nobel Prize winning physicist Niels Bohr)

Because stock markets have had a long history in the US, it is often US investors who have made their biggest mark. Nowadays, investing in stock markets is open to people in most countries. Here are five famous investors you can research further to learn from the best:

John (Jack) Bogle

We have this man to thank for the cheap ETFs (Exchange Traded Funds) that allow investors to invest in entire markets in exchange for no, or very low, fees.

Bogle pioneered the low-cost index fund, the Vanguard 500. This matches the *S&P 500*'s performance and charges a minimal fee to investors. From this humble beginning came the proliferation of ETFs make investing safer for beginner investors.

Bogle had 8 rules for investing:

☑ Choose funds with low costs.

☑ Buy a portfolio of funds, and hold onto it.

☑ Don't own too many funds.

☑ Beware of star managers.

☑ Keep an eye on assets that are very big.

☑ Use past performance to suss out risk.

☑ Just because a fund has done great in years gone by, does not mean it will again.

☑ If you are paying for an actively-managed fund, make sure you get your money's worth.

Warren Buffett

The 'Oracle of Omaha'. Buffett is the guy all investors want to be. He started investing with £174k and turned that into almost £100bn.

Buffett bought a textile making firm called Berkshire Hathaway in 1965. He turned it into a holding company for investments in insurance, energy and industrial firms. Tech is an area Buffett has shied away from; he only invests in what he knows, and newbie investors would do well to follow his example.

Berkshire Hathaway has produced an annual average return of 20% since 1965, doubling the performance of the S&P 500.

Buffett has an advantage over beginner investors. That advantage is that many of his success stories came from him personally intervening in companies he had invested in. His shareholdings gave him the leverage to introduce management and structural changes which then turned companies around.

Read all about Buffett in his biography *The Snowball: Warren Buffett and the Business of Life.*

Benjamin Graham

A pioneer, Graham invented the idea of value investing in the 1920s. This the idea that you look for stocks that are under-priced. The way to determine this is to analyse their financial fundamentals, and weigh up their prospects in their particular sector. Read all about value investing in Graham's classic 1949 book *The Intelligent Investor*.

Graham was in on an early example of 'shareholder activism' called the Northern Pipeline Affair. Shareholder activism is when shareholders use a big holding in a stock to push the management to adopt certain business strategies.

Graham had no time for market sentiment. Instead of trying to predict which way the market would swing, he concentrated only on analysing stocks. A good company, as far as he was concerned, was a good company — regardless of its current pricing.

Why you should really learn about Graham's work is the fact that he was the mentor to Warren Buffett and John Templeton.

Peter Lynch

Helmsman of the Fidelity Magellan Fund between 1977 and 1990, Lynch increased the fund's AUM (assets under management) from $20m to over £14bn. He chalked up an average annual return of 29%.

Read Lynch's tips and tricks in *One Up on Wall Street, Beating the Street* and *Learn to Earn.*

John Templeton

A mentee of Benjamin Graham, Templeton is a famous contrarian investor. That means he would do the opposite of what other investors were doing.

In 1939, Templeton bought 100 shares of every company traded on the NYSE that was worth less than $1.

34 of the 104 companies that Templeton bought into went bankrupt. But, from an investment of roughly $10k, he made $40k.

In 1954 he started his own mutual fund, the Templeton Growth Fund. This produced an annual return of 15%+ over 38 years.

WHEN INVESTMENTS GO WRONG

"It's not whether you're right or wrong that's important, but how much money you make when you're right and how much you lose when you're wrong."

(George Soros, billionaire and philanthropist)

As a beginner investor, you cannot be expected to get it right all the time. You cannot, in fact, be expected to get it right very often! That's why spreading your risk by investing in multiple assets is so important. Even the professionals get investing wrong, and often catastrophically.

Let us cast our eye over 7 financial scandals from history and see what we can learn ...

1. Too good to be true?

Event:	Attempted Sale of the Roman Empire
When?:	193AD
The villains:	Unidentified soldiers of the Pretorian Guard

What happened?

A Roman politician, Marcus Didius Julianus, bought the Roman Empire from top soldiers sworn to defend it — and ended up dead 66 days later. Some investment!

Stretching across Europe and parts of Asia, and running from 753 BC into the 5th century AD, the Roman Empire offers up plenty of tales of violence. 33 emperors, in all, were murdered or executed.

The year 193 AD saw two emperors go down. Emperor Pertinax was slain at the hands of the Pretorian Guard — Rome's top soldiers charged with defending the emperor.

This murder led to a unique bidding war for the Empire itself, as well as the death of the next emperor.

With Pertinax polished off, it was these elite soldiers that held the future of the entire Roman Empire in their hands. The decision was made to sell the entire empire to the highest bidder.

In return for the prize of the whole Roman Empire, the current Prefect of Rome, Titus Flavius Claudius Sulpicianus, promised every soldier 20,000 sesterces. But he was outbid by the proconsul of North Africa, Marcus Didius Julianus, who promised every Pretorian soldier 25,000 sesterces; this sum was almost six times their annual pay in one go!

The soldiers, unsurprisingly, opted for Julianus as Emperor. The Senate were bullied into agreeing.

Julianus' time at the top was a disaster. He was deeply unpopular for buying the empire. And the only thing he achieved was to devalue the Roman currency; over the long-run, this contributed to hyper-inflation and economic upheaval. Julianus was killed by a soldier on June 2nd, 193 AD.

The moral of the story

If it looks too good to be true, it probably is. This is a theme that underpins many financial scandals. The Pretorian Guard were never really in a position to sell the empire, because they never really owned it. Julianus thought he was getting deal of the millennium, but the deal was rotten to the core.

2. Tulip Mania – the first 'investment bubble'?

Event:	Ridiculous inflation in the price of particular flowers in Holland
When?:	1636-1637
The villains:	Nobody's fault – a market phenomenon

What happened?

Tulip Mania is often compared to the surge in popularity of cryptocurrencies.

An 'investment bubble' began to form around the trade in Dutch tulips, which were a unique luxury item. A futures market developed, in which, over the Spring, traders would agree to buy tulips at a certain price when they bloomed in April and May.

Between December 1636 and February 1637, prices went into a frenzy. Receipts have been found for a single tulip that cost the going rate for a nice house (5000 guilders). Then the bubble collapsed, and prices went back to normal.

Much has been written about 'Tulip Mania'.

A colourful and popular quote about Tulip Mania is provided by 19th Century historian C. Mackay in his *Memoirs of Extraordinary Popular Delusions and the Madness of Crowds*:

'Many individuals grew suddenly rich. A golden bait hung temptingly out before the people, and, one after the other, they rushed to the tulip marts, like flies around a honey-pot. Every one imagined that the passion for tulips would last for ever, and that the wealthy from every part of the world would send to Holland, and pay whatever prices were asked for them.'

Some modern historians, like Anne Goldgar, have pointed out that the bubble had little effect on the Dutch economy after it collapsed.

What we can be certain of is that investment bubbles do happen throughout history:

- ☑ Rational expectations amongst investors disappear.

- ☑ Investors flock to buy, purely because other investors are buying.

- ☑ Then investors realise they are holding an asset that is not actually worth much.

☑ Prices collapse, and investors get burnt.

The moral of the story

When there is hysteria in the air around investing, it is tempting to get involved. If you do so, be sure you are watching the markets like a hawk so you can get out before the crash.

3. If it looks too good to be true

Event:	The original 'Ponzi Scheme'
When?:	1918-1920
The villain:	Charles Ponzi

What happened?

The Ponzi Scheme is the template for pyramid schemes we see in the market nowadays.

With the original Ponzi scheme, a US businessman called Charles Ponzi promised profits of 50% in 45 days on an import scheme.

To pay off old investors with their promised profits, Ponzi simply used money from new investors. $200m in today's money was lost, and 6 banks collapsed as a result.

The moral of the story

As ever with investment scandals, it is easy to say in hindsight. But we are going to say it anyway: *if it looks too good to be true, it probably is!*

4. If you are in a hole, stop digging

Event:	Collapse of Barings Bank
When?:	1992-1995
The villain:	UK trader Nick Leeson

What happened?

Based in Singapore but working for UK Barings Bank, derivatives trader Nick Leeson lost £827m by hiding losses and trying to make them up with yet more loss-making trades. Barings Bank went bust as a result.

Leeson got a 6 year prison sentence in Changi Prison, Singapore for 'deceiving the bank's auditors and cheating the Singapore Exchange.'

With poetic justice, Leeson literally lost the jacket off his own back as a result of his crimes. His trading jacket was reportedly sold by Barings liquidators, KPMG, for £21,000 in 2007.

The moral of the story

What allowed Leeson to hide his mistakes was a lack of oversight. He was making up his own rules as he went along. And emotion got the better of him, with fear continually urging him on to gamble yet more in an effort to make good his losses.

This is a newbie mistake: make sure you don't fall into the same trap. When it comes to investment, *make a plan and stick to it.*

5. Corruption at the top ...

Event:	The Enron Scandal
When?:	2001
The villain:	Enron top executives

What happened?

Blue chip stock Enron — which claimed global revenues of $100bn in 2000 — stopped being a blue chip stock in 2001 when it turned out that accountants had been cooking the books. What's more, insider trading had been going on.

When the share price collapsed from $90 a share to virtually nothing, Enron investors lost $60bn. Enron president and CEO Jeffrey Skilling got a 24 year jail sentence. Accountancy giants Arthur Andersen were also found guilty of obstructing the course of justice, and their reputation never recovered.

The moral of the story

The late investment guru Philip Fisher advised investors to look for integrity in management teams. The Enron Scandal is why he was right. But how does the beginner investor know when a firm's management is playing fast and loose with the rules? After all, the financial world is full of firms riding close to the wind when it comes to regulation.

The way to avoid your investment funds going the way of Enron's reputation is to diversify your portfolio. You cannot be expected to know when a financial scandal is about to erupt. But you can make sure you have spread your investments so you will not lose everything in the event of crisis with one asset

6. So can we trust blue chip stocks?

Event:	The DieselGate Scandal
When?:	2008-2015
The villain:	Vehicle manufacturer Volkswagen

What happened?

In 2015, German vehicle manufacturer Volkswagen (VW) was found guilty by the US Environmental Protection Agency of having fixed some of the engines in their cars to only control harmful emissions when they were being tested in labs. 11m Volkswagens were thus being used by consumers whilst emitting harmful emissions without anybody realising.

This was a global scandal, with authorities from numerous countries taking action against VW. The VW share price dropped 40% in 2 weeks. Compared to the cryptocurrency sector, that's nothing. But VW was considered to be a blue chip stock, with an excellent range of products and a loyal global customer base.

The moral of the story

Spread your investments. Even the most respectable stocks can go sour.

7. Can we trust even the 'expert' investors?

Event:	UK celebrity Fund Manager goes bust
When?:	2019
The villain:	Neil Woodford

What happened?

In 2019, UK investment guru Neil Woodford had to suspend trading in his £3.7bn Woodford Equity Income fund. Hundreds of thousands of investors were caught on a sinking ship, with the value of their investment plummeting. £200m of investor funds remains trapped in the fund. The UK regulatory body, the FCA (Financial Conduct Authority), is investigating.

Prior to setting up his own (to-be-catastrophic) fund in 2014, Woodford had been a star fund manager, delivering returns of almost 3,000% over a quarter of a decade. But with Woodford Equity Income Fund, he picked stocks (like Purplebricks and motoring firm AA) that did not do well and invested in illiquid stocks that proved impossible to sell when he hit trouble. At its peak, Woodford's fund was worth over £10bn. It had lost £6bn rapidly when it ceased trading in 2019.

Woodford is trying to make a comeback with Jersey-based Woodford Capital Management. But his errors rocked the UK investment sector. And many investors lost their life savings with him. No wonder he is less than popular. His efforts have put a serious question mark to the whole issue of backing star fund managers; and new investors should take note.

The moral of the story

You can trust star investment gurus at one point in their career: when it is over! Who is to say that living investment legend Warren Buffett, worth now almost £100bn, will not lose it all? If you are going to invest with a fund manager, you will be expected to pay a fee commensurate with their reputation. But you may not get your money's worth. You may even get a disaster instead. They key, for the beginner investor, is to spread your investments.

CONCLUSION

'The future depends on what you do today'

(Spiritual guru Mahatma Gandhi)

Congratulations!

You have completed a whistle-stop tour of the options available to you for stock market investing.

You should now know:

- ☑ The importance of having a simple investment plan and sticking to it.

- ☑ Why you should always spread your risk.

- ☑ That a diversified portfolio is your starting point for spreading risk.

- ☑ That low-cost ETFs are the perfect choice for beginners to gain some stock exposure, as well as being a great way to avoid having to pick stocks yourself.

☑ That the first rule of choosing an online broker is finding one that deals with your country.

☑ That an unregulated broker is trouble waiting to happen.

☑ That value and growth investing — which means finding companies that have good growth prospects and are undervalued — has worked for some of the world's most successful investors.

☑ That even blue chip companies and star fund managers can lose your money. And that's why diversification is so important.

Thanks to the rise of online brokers, the financial markets present exciting opportunities which will only expand over time. It is great news that commissions on trades are becoming less popular — but watch out for spreads!

A final piece of advice in general: be realistic.

Be realistic that, if you are seeking high-risk investments like cryptos, you can quickly lose all your money.

Be realistic that, if an investment does not go your way, you can learn from your mistake and move on. Take the pressure off yourself. As investors, we are not fortune-tellers. We cannot always get it right.

Be realistic too that the only way to secure gains with some safety is to invest over the long-term.

Be realistic that money makes money. The beginning of your investment journey may be challenging, without much to show for your teething period financially. But, once you have got going, you may be pleasantly surprised where you end up in a few years time. Then, you will have the capital to develop your skills, as well as have the capital to make your wins bigger: this forward cycle is how the great investors have made billions.

Good luck. Keep emotion out of it. Stick to your investment plan.

DISCLAIMER

This book contains opinions and ideas of the author and is meant to teach the reader informative and helpful knowledge while due care should be taken by the user in the application of the information provided. The instructions and strategies are possibly not right for every reader and there is no guarantee that they work for everyone. Using this book and implementing the information/recipes therein contained is explicitly your own responsibility and risk. This work with all its contents, does not guarantee correctness, completion, quality or correctness of the provided information. Misinformation or misprints cannot be completely eliminated.

Printed in Great Britain
by Amazon

79672553R10064